Joseph and the Plates

written by Tiffany Thomas
illustrated by Nikki Casassa

CFI • An imprint of Cedar Fort, Inc. • Springville, Utah

HARD WORDS:
Joseph, church, angel

PARENT TIP: Words that begin with "wh" can be tricky. Instead of sounding them out, have them become sight words to memorize.

This is Joseph.
He is born 1,500
years after Moroni.

There are a lot of churches.

Joseph prays to know
which church is right.

God and Jesus come to Joseph.

Jesus says none of
the churches are right.

Later, Joseph prays again.

Moroni comes.
Moroni is an angel.

Moroni tells Joseph where to find the plates.

Joseph finds
the plates.

He makes the words into English.

This is the Book of Mormon.

The end.

This is not an official publication of The Church of Jesus Christ of Latter-day Saints. The opinions and views expressed herein belong solely to the author and do not necessarily represent the opinions or views of Cedar Fort, Inc. Permission for the use of sources, graphics, and photos is also solely the responsibility of the author.

ISBN 13: 978-1-4621-4337-5

Published by CFI, an imprint of Cedar Fort, Inc. • 2373 W. 700 S., Suite 100, Springville, UT 84663
Distributed by Cedar Fort, Inc., www.cedarfort.com

Cover design and interior layout design by Shawnda T. Craig
Cover design © 2022 Cedar Fort, Inc.
Printed in China • Printed on acid-free paper
10 9 8 7 6 5 4 3 2 1